Beyond the Compass

Learning to See the Unseen

Dave Wager

Intimate **WARRIOR** SERIES

Foreword by Dave Abbatacola

Grace Acres Press
P.O. Box 22
Larkspur, CO 80118
888-700-GRACE (4722)
(303) 681-9995
(303) 681-9996 fax
www.GraceAcresPress.com

CULTIVATING JOY

Throughout this book, we use the following abbreviations:
NIV *New International Version*
Scripture taken from the *Holy Bible, New International Version.*®
NIV.® Copyright © 1973, 1978, 1984 by International Bible
Society. Used by permission of Zondervan Publishing House.
All rights reserved.

NLT *New Living Testament*
Holy Bible, New Living Translation. Copyright © 1996
by Tyndale Charitable Trust. All rights reserved. Database
copyright © 1997 NavPress Software.

Library of Congress Cataloging-in-Publication Data:

ISBN: 978-1-60265-002-2

Printed in the United States of America
10 09 08 07   01 02 03 04 05 06 07 08 09 10

Praise for *Beyond the Compass*

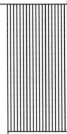

*An important part of spiritual maturity is recognizing
the presence of God, right here, right now. Dave Wager's
reflections and directional exercises in this book help us
develop eyes to see what we otherwise would miss: the
work of God in each of our days.*

MARSHALL SHELLEY
Vice President, Editorial
Christianity Today International

---

*The friends I enjoy the most are the ones who cause me
to think. Dave Wager's book,* Beyond the Compass, *has
become such a friend to me. With poignant insights and
fascinating questions, this book helps me think outside the
box but never outside the Truth. In reading it, I find myself
sometimes confessing my sin, sometimes repenting of my
ways, and always wanting more of the reality of God in
my life. I can't think of another book, besides the Bible, so
succinctly written, that has led me to ponder so long and
so deeply about those things that are most significant.*

ROY HANSCHKE
Morning Show Host and Church
Relations Director, KPOF Radio

---

*With keen insight and quick wit, Dave Wager has gathered
readable thoughts on Christian life and practical theology.
Wager's true-north "truths" are profound, repeatable, and
poignant. This book is a pleasant and moving experience.*

KIM SKATTUM
Pastor, Crossroads Church
Northglenn, Colorado

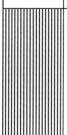

Dave Wager answers questions that many of us think about, but are afraid to ask. In so doing, he provides refreshing insights from Scripture and a window into his life—his lifelong pursuit of walking intimately with God. Conditioned by his leadership in the community of a Christian camp and conference center, you'll find Dave's thoughts practical, challenging, and riddled with inspiration. I highly recommend the book.

BOB KOBIELUSH
President
Christian Camp and Conference
Association

There are plenty of devotionals, but not enough devotion. Dave's work will stir in us the devotion that all Christians can have when we get our sense of direction pointed toward the unseen, yet very real, activity in the heavenly realm. A quick glance at a compass will help the traveler find the way and arrive at the right destination. Dave's daily thoughts don't take long to read, but they point us in the right direction. This devotional moves the reader further into spiritual living for a more devout relationship with the invisible God.

DAN HETTINGER
Founder
The Jakin Group

This book is dedicated to my mom, Joyce Wager,
in appreciation for the many occasions on which she
encouraged and supported me as I walked beyond
the compass.

Never let us despair. God's time for mercy will come; yea, it has come, if our time for believing has arrived.

—C. H. Spurgeon

Contents

About the Author   ix

Foreword   xi

Acknowledgments   xiii

Introduction   xv

Thought for Day 1   2

*How much do you need to understand before you believe?
Can you believe something and not understand it?*

Thought for Day 2   6

*Does God have an opinion or perspective? Is my world
really what I think it is?*

Thought for Day 3   10

*What are the angels doing today? Is God really active
in my life, or is He at a distance?*

Thought for Day 4   14

*How do I know that I am not a false teacher? What
outside criterion do I use to honestly evaluate my life?*

Thought for Day 5   18

What does it mean to be blessed of God?

Thought for Day 6   22

*What does faith actually look like? What in my life
demonstrates that I have faith?*

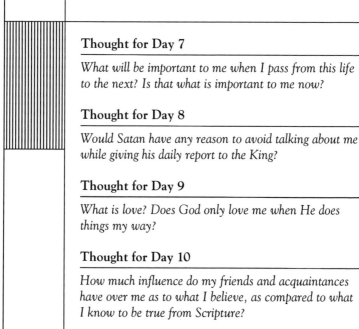

Thought for Day 7 26

What will be important to me when I pass from this life to the next? Is that what is important to me now?

Thought for Day 8 30

Would Satan have any reason to avoid talking about me while giving his daily report to the King?

Thought for Day 9 34

What is love? Does God only love me when He does things my way?

Thought for Day 10 38

How much influence do my friends and acquaintances have over me as to what I believe, as compared to what I know to be true from Scripture?

Thought for Day 11 42

Who is responsible for what I believe?

Thought for Day 12 46

What acceptable ways have I given Satan to deceive me with?

Thought for Day 13 50

Do I actually lead when I know what is right, or do I give in to keep the (apparent) peace?

Thought for Day 14 54

God is sovereign, so isn't He responsible for my actions?

Thought for Day 15   58

*Am I allowing God to do anything in my life that will
prove to those around me that He is God and that I am
His servant?*

Thought for Day 16   62

*What would I need to know and believe to allow me
to march boldly to my death rather than recant what
I believe?*

Thought for Day 17   66

*How important is talking with God? How much have
I talked with Him today?*

Thought for Day 18   70

*What in my life would cause Jesus to get up off
His throne in excited anticipation of what was about
to happen?*

Thought for Day 19   74

*Why has God given you your position, assets, talents,
and health?*

Thought for Day 20   78

Why is it so hard to understand what God says?

Thought for Day 21   82

*After my life on earth is over, will God allow me to
be with Him forever? How do I know?*

Final Thoughts   86

About the Author

For the past twenty-five years, Dave Wager has served as a leader, friend, and teacher to thousands who have entered the educational grounds of Silver Birch Ranch in White Lake, Wisconsin. Today Dave continues to serve as the president of Silver Birch Ranch, and also teaches at camps, conferences, churches, and businesses throughout the world.

Dave's life has been dedicated to the growth of young people, first as a volunteer youth worker and then later as a fifth-grade teacher. He has served as president of the Wisconsin Christian Camping Association and currently teaches a class in "Christian Life and Ethics" at the Nicolet Bible Institute. Dave holds a B.A. from Wheaton College and an M.S. Ed. from Northern Illinois University.

Dave desires that each person he meets walk intimately with God and fulfill the purposes for which he or she was designed. He believes that joy and effectiveness in life, work, and ministry come from knowing what really matters. His focus is in examining how today's choices affect the real bottom line: knowing what we are about, what are our responsibilities, and what are God's responsibilities.

Foreword

I know of only one person who longs for people to have intimacy with God more than Dave Wager, and that is God Himself. Dave's life, ministry, marriage, parenting, and all the other aspects of his self: all reflect a man's heart that beats for God and desires others to have that same longing.

I have known Dave Wager since I was a young child attending the church where his father ministered. Dave was one of my first Sunday School teachers. He led the children's ministry I eventually attended. Throughout the years, our paths have also crossed at Silver Birch Ranch, where I have served in various capacities over a thirty-year period; Dave has been the president of Silver Birch for many of those years. During that time span, Dave's mission has not changed: Know Jesus and get others to know and be awed by this Jesus! Whether Dave and I talked horses, camping, the Green Bay Packers, or the workings of the universe, all the conversations eventually ended up linked to God's overall purpose for His Creation.

Dave spends time with God and wants others to do so as well.

Dave understands the superficiality of our culture: how most of it, most of the time, gives little attention to God. So Dave goes the other way. He directs and devotes his

time, thoughts, passions, a vibrant camp ministry, his family life (consisting of his wife, Linda, and their two daughters), a growing college program, and everything else toward pleasing God and knowing His ways. And he wants others to do so as well.

The premise of *Beyond the Compass* is not rocket science. If you want to know God, you must spend time with Him. If you want brokenness and humility, which God requires, spend time with Him. If you want a fulfilled life, spend time with Him. If you desire joy and hope and peace in a chaotic world, spend time with God. If you need guidance and direction, spend time with our Lord. Time well spent with Abba Father can restore your soul, revive your spirit, and comfort, enlighten, and guide your life.

The apostle Paul commanded the Ephesians to find out what pleases the Lord. That mission is not too difficult for us. Truth can be known and understood, and ultimately it will set us free. Dave understands this, and this fact is reflected in his life and work. This book will help you get on the way to understanding what will please the Lover of your soul and create a greater hunger for Him and His Word!

April 2007   Dave Abbatacola
                                      Senior Pastor
                                      Gold Canyon Community
                                      Church

Acknowledgments

I am grateful to those faithful volunteer workers who have given their time and resources to make Silver Birch Ranch a reality. Their willingness to walk beyond the compass has helped shape my life and thinking in ways for which I will be forever thankful.

Introduction

Proverbs 3:5 (NLT)

5 TRUST IN THE LORD WITH ALL YOUR HEART; DO NOT DEPEND ON YOUR OWN UNDERSTANDING.

Satan's greatest weapon in the war against humankind is deception. Because he is older than we are and smarter than we are, he often uses his experience and know-how to encourage us to adamantly believe that we are going in the right direction when in fact we are headed down a path toward destruction. Each of us, no matter how disciplined, has a tendency to lie to ourselves; to not see clearly what is really going on; to spin facts and details to match our own (limited) understanding; to think that we are headed north when we are really going south.

What an intimate warrior must do is meet with our King on a regular basis and learn to accept and apply what He says, for He alone cannot and will not be fooled. God alone is our "true north"; all other directions in life can and ultimately must be evaluated by His absolutes. In short, we must move beyond the compass and make God the only direction and goal in our lives.

This book is designed to help you hear the voice of God and, possibly, to see what you have never seen before. It is our desire that you dedicate one hour a day for twenty-one days to reading the Scripture passages and short commentaries in this book. Then, we ask you to sit (perhaps with a good cup of coffee), think, and record your thoughts.

There is no way you can even begin to understand the incomprehensible without long periods of tremendous pondering. Satan will do all he can to keep you from meeting with God, because your intimacy with God and your obedience to God are the only things Satan really fears.

I encourage you not only to get into the habit of sitting alone with God, but also to begin to encourage others to do the same. Let us continue to urge Christians every-where to spend time with God. Let's ask God to give us one million men and women in our country who become dedicated to spending a minimum of an hour each day pondering the truths of the Scriptures. Let God use you to start a movement—in your family, neighborhood, and state—of individuals who know God, obey God, and make His ways known.

At the end of each daily thought in this book, you will see a "True North" statement. This statement recognizes something that is absolute: something that you must adjust your life to, rather than adjusting it according to your life, comprehension, or convenience.

May God's Spirit guide your thoughts as you read, think, pray, and respond to His Word.

Thought for Day 1

How much do you need to understand before you believe? Can you believe something and not understand it?

Romans 11:33–36 (NIV)

33 OH, THE DEPTH OF THE RICHES OF THE WISDOM AND KNOWLEDGE OF GOD! HOW UNSEARCHABLE HIS JUDGMENTS, AND HIS PATHS BEYOND TRACING OUT!

34 "WHO HAS KNOWN THE MIND OF THE LORD? OR WHO HAS BEEN HIS COUNSELOR?"

35 "WHO HAS EVER GIVEN TO GOD, THAT GOD SHOULD REPAY HIM?"

36 FOR FROM HIM AND THROUGH HIM AND TO HIM ARE ALL THINGS. TO HIM BE THE GLORY FOREVER! AMEN.

Ephesians 3:8 (NIV)

8 ALTHOUGH I AM LESS THAN THE LEAST OF ALL GOD'S PEOPLE, THIS GRACE WAS GIVEN ME: TO PREACH TO THE GENTILES THE UNSEARCHABLE RICHES OF CHRIST....

Unsearchable is quite an interesting word. This word, which could literally mean "beyond tracing out" or even "incapable of being followed by footprints," is used only in these two passages, in all of Scripture.

What does this mean? What could this mean? Could it mean that God's dumbest thought is smarter than my smartest thought? Yes. Could it mean that even after God works, I may not be able to fully comprehend how he worked? Yes. Could it mean that there is much going on in the world (in the universe!) that I just do not or cannot understand? Yes.

Many times, we seem to get lost in our own understanding. We work in the realm of human thinking, human wisdom, and human advice so much of the time that it becomes normal to think humanly. There may be nothing wrong with being human, but we will miss a lot if we continue to live by human rather than divine thinking.

Today, there is a battle going on. Today, God is at work. Today, Satan is hatching a scheme. Today, people will die for their faith, abandon their faith, and begin their faith. Today, there will be rejoicing in heaven over those who repent of their sins, and amazement at those who have the very power and Word of God at their disposal yet do not use it. Today, much will happen indeed.

Will I be a part of this, or will I miss it? Will I be engaged in the eternal struggle, or just try to make it to the end of the day? Will my goal be one of being an active soldier for our King, or will I not even be aware of the war and what is at stake?

There is much that is happening today, and when it is all over, even if I am an active participant, I may not be able to see clearly all that God has accomplished.

God, help me today to see what your agenda is and how I might be a part of such a wonderful, unimaginable, and comprehensive plan!

 True North: God's dumbest thought is smarter than my smartest thought.

Lord, you have blessed me beyond my wildest imigination! Please help me enjoy and be greatful for what you've given me. To be generous and share my blessings. Deliver me from feelings of guilt for what I have but rather be a good steward recognizing it all belongs to you and I am only the priviledged steward.

I want to Trust, obey and be faithful to you at all times and in every way! I want to be rich in the wisdom and knowledge of God!

Thought for Day 2

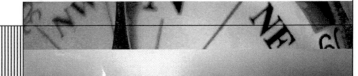

Does God have an opinion or perspective?
Is my world really what I think it is?

Proverbs 3:5–6 (NIV)

5 TRUST IN THE LORD WITH ALL YOUR HEART AND LEAN
NOT ON YOUR OWN UNDERSTANDING;

6 IN ALL YOUR WAYS ACKNOWLEDGE HIM, AND HE WILL
MAKE YOUR PATHS STRAIGHT.

How am I supposed to do this?

I realize that I am not that bright, but really, when it
comes right down to it, my understanding is all I've got.
I understand certain things about the universe, my
country, my neighborhood, my work, my family, and
myself. I understand a bit about how to take care of a
car, house, lawn, and boat. I spend time with God and
know a bit about who He is and how He works. Yet,
my understanding always seems so finite. It seems as if
I can always learn more; sometimes what I learn even
negates what I thought I already knew.

I remember talking with a scientist who is a Christian
who was telling me about a discussion he had had with
some scientists who did not know Christ and would not
acknowledge God. He said that these scientists spent
their lives trying to understand the universe (or their
specialty parts of the universe). When they got together,
they spoke of things they understood and spoke of these

things with the certainty that comes from hours of study and debate. These scientists were always willing to share what they knew with other people, and to wow others with facts, charts, big words, and conclusions.

The problem is that these scientists also exposed a major flaw in their system of gaining knowledge. By their own admission, the facts in their field change and new data become available. The consequence is that what was believed to be absolute truth 150 years ago became nonsense just 100 years ago, because of the new information the scientific community had gleaned from new studies, technology, and experimentation. Even fifty years ago, the "facts" were different from what they are today, for the same reason.

Following this pattern, what can we assume about the future for these scientists? We can and must assume that as new "facts" are discovered, the old "facts" will be disproven and rendered "nonfacts." The old understanding will be proven deficient and former "knowledge" will be discarded or revamped.

In the end, when all things stop, every scientist will stand before the I Am and realize the truth. God has not changed. His facts have not changed. If you start with that which never changes, even if you do not understand it all, you at least start with the right information. My understanding is limited; God's is not. I am continually learning; God is not. I have an opinion; God does not. I have a perspective; God does not.

I very much want to make God like me so that I can understand Him, yet I must not. The best I can do is spend time admitting that my understanding is limited, and realizing that the time I actually understand the most is when I finally admit that I do not understand and yield my life to the only One who does.

Isaiah 55:8 (NIV)

8 "For my thoughts are not your thoughts, neither are your ways my ways," declares the Lord.

True North: God has no opinions or perspective.

_____

_____

_____

_____

_____

_____

_____

_____

_____

_____

_____

_____

Thought for Day 3

What are the angels doing today? Is God really active in my life, or is He at a distance?

2 Kings 6:15–17 (NIV)

15 When the servant of the man of God got up and went out early the next morning, an army with horses and chariots had surrounded the city. "Oh, my lord, what shall we do?" the servant asked.

16 "Don't be afraid," the prophet answered. "Those who are with us are more than those who are with them."

17 And Elisha prayed, "O Lord, open his eyes so he may see." Then the Lord opened the servant's eyes, and he looked and saw the hills full of horses and chariots of fire all around Elisha.

I am not sure that I would have been as calm as Elisha in the same situation. I am not sure that my prayer would have been the same as Elisha's. In fact, if there were an army parked outside my house ready to kill me, and (I assume) my wife, family, and anyone else who had taken shelter in my home, I might have prayed for something other than for my servant's eyes to be opened. This has to be one of the most bizarre prayers in the Bible . . . or is it?

The real question must be: What does Elisha understand? What does he see that I am missing? For some reason, when impending tragedy was at his door, his concern was to show all those involved who God was. He did not ask for deliverance. He did not ask for peace or comfort or for lightning to come down from heaven to destroy his enemies. All he asked was that his servant's eyes be opened so that the servant could see what God was really doing.

So many times in life, I may be asking God for the wrong thing. So often I ask Him to remove me from a controversy or to heal the disease or to take away the discomfort. I do not know if I ever just asked Him to open my eyes and let me see His plan, His protection, His love, His mercy, or His kindness. Even more shocking is that I probably never prayed that God would open up the eyes of those around me to see Him through my impending doom.

This prayer of Elisha's was one gutsy prayer . . . or was it?

Could it be that Elisha was so close, so intimate with God that this was normal prayer, his normal response? Could anyone be so close to God that in all circumstances of life their concern is revealing God rather than being comfortable? Could anyone today be so close to God that they actually know what He and His angels are up to?

Obviously the answer is yes. When Jesus was on earth, he told His disciples that it would be good for Him to leave, for when He did, they would receive the Holy Spirit, who would be able to guide them, direct them, pray for them, and otherwise "indwell" them. The idea of God being with you 24/7/365 was a positive thing to Jesus, even though He limited this type of arrangement until after He left (except for special assignments, like Elisha and others in the Old Testament).

Today, God desires me to know what I must know to be relevant in His war. Today, the Holy Spirit of God indwells me, so I am capable of seeing and understanding the world and the universe the way God sees and understands. Today, God will use the circumstances of my life to reveal to the world who He is and what He is about.

Do I get it? Do I see it? Do I even want any part in it?

True North: God and His angels are active in His service and plans today, all day, every day.

_____

_____

_____

_____

_____

_____

_____

_____

_____

_____

_____

_____

Thought for Day 4

How do I know that I am not a false teacher?
What outside criterion do I use to honestly
evaluate my life?

Jude 1:8–10 (NIV)

8 IN THE VERY SAME WAY, THESE DREAMERS POLLUTE
THEIR OWN BODIES, REJECT AUTHORITY AND SLANDER
CELESTIAL BEINGS.

9 BUT EVEN THE ARCHANGEL MICHAEL, WHEN HE WAS
DISPUTING WITH THE DEVIL ABOUT THE BODY OF MOSES,
DID NOT DARE TO BRING A SLANDEROUS ACCUSATION
AGAINST HIM, BUT SAID, "THE LORD REBUKE YOU!"

10 YET THESE MEN SPEAK ABUSIVELY AGAINST WHAT-
EVER THEY DO NOT UNDERSTAND; AND WHAT THINGS
THEY DO UNDERSTAND BY INSTINCT, LIKE UNREASONING
ANIMALS—THESE ARE THE VERY THINGS THAT DESTROY
THEM.

The book of Jude is all about false teachers, and should
be studied by all who truly want to know that they are
on the right team. The characteristics that Jude describes
in this very short book are there so that we can judge
ourselves and others as to their actual family status. The
ultimate judgment belongs to God, yet I must have
some evaluatory standards that I use to discern to whom
I will listen and whom I will ignore. Jude helps me by
outlining such a criterion.

One of the most fascinating things about the book of Jude is the comment this author makes concerning Michael, the archangel. Jude talks about a time in history when Michael, the archangel, argued with Satan over the very body of Moses. Jude talks of this encounter as if it were common knowledge. He seems to use this example, because it is obviously so well known and well understood, to talk about how false teachers minimize the things they do not understand.

In fact, he says that there will be false teachers who teach only things they can understand. Because this angel-warfare business is not front and center in their thinking, they minimize it, make fun of it, or even deny it.

Story after story in the Bible shows us that much is happening that we do not understand. I am not sure what happened after Moses died, but I do know that the angels went to battle over the eventual result. I do not know why God did not just say something and stop the battle. I am not sure why the body of Moses would matter to anyone. The only thing I am sure of is that Michael, the archangel, and Satan battled for it.

Today, I wonder what else I am not certain of just because I am so locked into thinking like a human. I know that I have been guilty of making fun of or minimizing things I do not understand, and that as I get older the amount I do not understand grows at a greater rate than the amount I do understand.

The only solace I have is that the One I love, the One who controls the universe, the One who is, and was, and is to come, is my Father. He is older than I am, smarter than I am, and loves me. I can trust Him.

God, open my eyes to your work and your ways today and forgive me for trying to fit your ways, your universe, and your plan into my understanding.

True North: There is much going on that I am totally unaware of. I am not the center of the universe.

_____

_____

_____

_____

_____

_____

_____

_____

_____

_____

_____

_____

_____

_____

Thought for Day 5

What does it mean to be blessed of God?

Hebrews 11:32–35a (NIV)

32 AND WHAT MORE SHALL I SAY? I DO NOT HAVE TIME TO TELL ABOUT GIDEON, BARAK, SAMSON, JEPHTHAH, DAVID, SAMUEL AND THE PROPHETS,

33 WHO THROUGH FAITH CONQUERED KINGDOMS, ADMINISTERED JUSTICE, AND GAINED WHAT WAS PROMISED; WHO SHUT THE MOUTHS OF LIONS,

34 QUENCHED THE FURY OF THE FLAMES, AND ESCAPED THE EDGE OF THE SWORD; WHOSE WEAKNESS WAS TURNED TO STRENGTH; AND WHO BECAME POWERFUL IN BATTLE AND ROUTED FOREIGN ARMIES.

35A WOMEN RECEIVED BACK THEIR DEAD, RAISED TO LIFE AGAIN.

What a group! I want to be identified with them! I want to be one who conquers kingdoms, administers justice, gains what is promised, and shuts the mouths of lions. I want to be one who gets to quench the fury of the flames, escape the edge of the sword, and see the impossible happen through me—even though I am totally unable to make it happen. I want to be powerful in battle and see the enemy run for their lives when I peek out of my foxhole. I want to see people's lives changed, even

to the point where they are brought back from the dead!
What a life!

Hebrews 11:35b–40 (NIV)

35B OTHERS WERE TORTURED AND REFUSED TO
BE RELEASED, SO THAT THEY MIGHT GAIN A BETTER
RESURRECTION.

36 SOME FACED JEERS AND FLOGGING, WHILE STILL
OTHERS WERE CHAINED AND PUT IN PRISON.

37 THEY WERE STONED; THEY WERE SAWED IN TWO; THEY
WERE PUT TO DEATH BY THE SWORD. THEY WENT ABOUT
IN SHEEPSKINS AND GOATSKINS, DESTITUTE, PERSECUTED
AND MISTREATED—

38 THE WORLD WAS NOT WORTHY OF THEM. THEY
WANDERED IN DESERTS AND MOUNTAINS, AND IN CAVES
AND HOLES IN THE GROUND.

39 THESE WERE ALL COMMENDED FOR THEIR FAITH, YET
NONE OF THEM RECEIVED WHAT HAD BEEN PROMISED.

40 GOD HAD PLANNED SOMETHING BETTER FOR US SO
THAT ONLY TOGETHER WITH US WOULD THEY BE MADE
PERFECT.

I am not sure I want to be a part of this group. That first
group sounded better to me. Their lives seemed exciting,
victorious, even exhilarating. What I do understand
from this is that my faith is what counts, not my human
accomplishments. Today, there will be people who give
their lives for the King and His work and ways. They will
look like losers when in reality they are winners. They

will look like they wasted their lives when in reality they were more a part of the game than I will ever be.

Father, forgive me for thinking in such . . ."Western" ways. Somehow I think I am blessed when my bills are paid, the enemy runs, my loved ones are rescued, and my Red Seas part. In reality, you have made it clear that my faith may take me to the very limits of my human understanding. My faith and obedience may require me to live in a way that makes me look like a loser to my people.

It is not for me to say what my job is. It is not for me to ask God to allow me to be in category one instead of category two. It is for me to ask that God make Himself and His ways so clear to me that I would rather die honorably than live and dishonor His name or His ways. I will be dead a whole lot longer than I will ever be alive, and I need to see that my time on this earth is my investment period, not my retirement period. I need to see God and be willing to let Him do as He wishes with my life, my resources, and my talents. This may lead to my death, or it may lead to a national revival. That is not up to me. I must live in the realm of what is up to me. Help me, God!

 True North: I can be constantly blessed by God and still be sick, hurt, poor, persecuted, and uncomfortable.

Job 16:19-22

_____

_____

_____

Thought for Day 6

What does faith actually look like? What in my life demonstrates that I have faith?

Hebrews 11:39–40 (NLT)

39 ALL OF THESE PEOPLE WE HAVE MENTIONED RECEIVED GOD'S APPROVAL BECAUSE OF THEIR FAITH, YET NONE OF THEM RECEIVED ALL THAT GOD HAD PROMISED.

40 FOR GOD HAD FAR BETTER THINGS IN MIND FOR US THAT WOULD ALSO BENEFIT THEM, FOR THEY CAN'T RECEIVE THE PRIZE AT THE END OF THE RACE UNTIL WE FINISH THE RACE.

All people, throughout history, will be judged according to their faith. This principle is made quite clear throughout Scripture, and we would be wise to evaluate our lives by the same premise by which God will one day evaluate us.

There is a part of this passage from Hebrews that gives us a glimpse as to what has happened to all those whom God did consider faithful. Obviously, the faithful were not necessarily given a life of ease, comfort, and human success. In fact, ease, comfort, and human success often eluded those who really loved and listened to God. Yet, the fact in the Scriptures that is quite clear is that one day God wins—and all those who trusted in Him and obeyed Him will win as well.

What is interesting in these last verses in the "faith chapter" is the use of the words *us* and *them*. There were many who finished their lives faithful yet did not receive all that was promised; these verses tell us what this "many" are up to today. We are told that those who were faithful, those who did right, have something great in store for them that involves us!

I remember watching the Winter Olympics on television and taking a keen interest in the four-man cross-country ski race. In this particular year, the Italians were challenging the ever-dominant Norwegians, and the media was having a field day with this old but powerful rivalry. As I turned on the television, I saw that three out of the four Italians were finished with the race, and stood at the finish line cheering on the final skier. Each Italian skier realized that no matter what his role, no matter what his sacrifice, no matter what his skill, no matter how big a lead he gained, none of them won until the final racer finished the race in first place. At that moment, and not until then, they and the nation of Italy would win and the celebration could begin.

The author of Hebrews has said the same about the race of life. We are told that those who have gone before us are now witnesses to the races we are running. They could be witnesses to the most private moments of our lives, to how we use our money, to how we use our time and what we say or do not say. They are, in a way, cheering us on, for they do not win until we win.

What is really going on? Who is really involved? Who is really watching? What are they really seeing? What part am I really playing?

I am not absolutely sure. The thing I am sure about is that those whom God considered faithful and are now

gone from this earth are going to cheer for me today.
This could include my dad, Moses, Elijah, and others.
I wonder if they will have anything to cheer about today,
or if today a collective groan will be sounded that comes
from the agony of defeat?

I have choices each day, as long as I am alive. I can be
a part of that group someday: that group of the faithful,
or just a citizen of Italy, so to speak. For now, the choice
is mine.

> **True North: There is a host in heaven watching
> and cheering those who are left to fight on the
> earth.**

Thought for Day 7

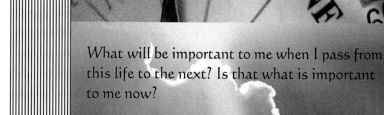

What will be important to me when I pass from this life to the next? Is that what is important to me now?

Luke 16:19–24 (NIV)

19 There was a rich man who was dressed in purple and fine linen and lived in luxury every day.

20 At his gate was laid a beggar named Lazarus, covered with sores

21 And longing to eat what fell from the rich man's table. Even the dogs came and licked his sores.

22 The time came when the beggar died and the angels carried him to Abraham's side. The rich man also died and was buried.

23 In hell, where he was in torment, he looked up and saw Abraham far away, with Lazarus by his side.

24 So he called to him, "Father Abraham, have pity on me and send Lazarus to dip the tip of his finger in water and cool my tongue, because I am in agony in this fire."

This is a most interesting passage, in that it gives us a glimpse of what really goes on after this life is over. This story, as told to us by Jesus, is a firsthand account of what actually happens when we die. The ultimate end of the story revolves around the fact that the rich man's only real concern in hell (other than a moment of personal relief) was that somehow or someway his brothers would be told of the reality that will indeed come to them. The rich man wanted somehow to shock his family out of their self-absorbed lives and make them really understand that heaven and hell are real, that they are forever, that the wrath of God is something you do not want to experience.

As interesting as that part of the story is, the most interesting part of the story may be what happens to one who loves God at the moment of death. Jesus makes it clear—and He would know!—that when the poor person died, he was met and carried by angels to be with God. The poor man was the one who had time for, took time for, and developed a relationship with God.

In contrast, when the rich man died there was no one there, at least in this revelation, to meet him. Instead, the next line reveals that he is "in hell."

What a difference between what happens to those who die in the Lord and those who do not! Those who die in Christ have a party, a reunion of sorts, a welcome-home adventure, carried by angels to the King. We are not left alone. We are not left to wonder. We are never really dead.

What is really going on is a victory parade of sorts. What is really going on is the guarding of our beings by the protection of our King. What is really going on is the real beginning of the end—and we already know the ending, the victory that awaits those who align with the King.

I am not sure which angels do the carrying. Perhaps it is our "guardian" angels; perhaps it is angels on special assignment; perhaps there is an actual angel or squadron of angels of death. All I know for sure is that at and during the scariest time of human existence, God will make certain that His own are cared for, calmed, and reassured.

That is what is really going on. That is too wonderful for me to grasp.

True North: When I die, I will either be carried or buried.

_____

_____

_____

_____

_____

_____

_____

_____

_____

_____

_____

_____

Thought for Day 8

Would Satan have any reason to avoid talking about me while giving his daily report to the King?

Job 1:6–8 (NIV)

6 ONE DAY THE ANGELS CAME TO PRESENT THEMSELVES BEFORE THE LORD, AND SATAN ALSO CAME WITH THEM.

7 THE LORD SAID TO SATAN, "WHERE HAVE YOU COME FROM?" SATAN ANSWERED THE LORD, "FROM ROAMING THROUGH THE EARTH AND GOING BACK AND FORTH IN IT."

8 THEN THE LORD SAID TO SATAN, "HAVE YOU CONSIDERED MY SERVANT JOB? THERE IS NO ONE ON EARTH LIKE HIM; HE IS BLAMELESS AND UPRIGHT, A MAN WHO FEARS GOD AND SHUNS EVIL."

Job, most likely the oldest book in the Bible, gives us great insight into what is really happening. For some reason, God wanted us to know what was going on behind the scenes. I am sure that Job would have benefited from knowing what was going on, but that knowledge was not for him. Instead, God gave this record to us so that we can see how God has chosen to work and what is really going on.

It is interesting that here Satan is shown as one who roams the earth and reports back to God. This is certainly consistent with how he is portrayed in Scripture, as a roaring lion or an accuser. In this case, it seems that in

Satan's report on the tragic men and women of the earth, he skipped a man, a man named Job.

If I glean anything from this book of Job, I can extrapolate that there is indeed a battle. This battle is not necessarily about me, but it does involve or concern me. The battle is really between God and Satan. However, because I am loved by God, and because God has given me choice, Satan has targeted me as his only opportunity to "hurt" God.

Satan, like any lion, really works at finding the weakling, the loner, the one who has been separated from the herd. When he finds those who have been separated, he works them over, tires them out, and eventually pounces and destroys them.

---

1 Peter 5:8 (NIV)

8 BE SELF-CONTROLLED AND ALERT. YOUR ENEMY THE DEVIL PROWLS AROUND LIKE A ROARING LION LOOKING FOR SOMEONE TO DEVOUR.

The oldest lesson we are to learn from the oldest book in the Bible is the fact that Satan is on the prowl; that Satan opposes God; that Satan is trying to use me as an example of failure to God. The oldest lesson in Scripture is the lesson that I am really on display, somehow, some way, and for some reason.

Today, in the heavenly realm, I can be used as an example of one who has faith or one who lacks faith. I can be one who was cheered for or one who has disgusted the heavenly host.

Today, I have the choice to recognize what is really going on or pretend that nothing is going on.

God, forgive me for so often forgetting the purposes of life, the war that is so real, and the consequences that are everlasting.

True North: Satan is looking for a way to destroy me today.

Thought for Day 9

What is love? Does God only love me when He does things my way?

Job 1:8–12 (NIV)

8 Then the Lord said to Satan, "Have you considered my servant Job? There is no one on earth like him; he is blameless and upright, a man who fears God and shuns evil."

9 "Does Job fear God for nothing?" Satan replied.

10 "Have you not put a hedge around him and his household and everything he has? You have blessed the work of his hands, so that his flocks and herds are spread throughout the land.

11 But stretch out your hand and strike everything he has, and he will surely curse you to your face."

12 The Lord said to Satan, "Very well, then, everything he has is in your hands, but on the man himself do not lay a finger." Then Satan went out from the presence of the Lord.

What is it that Satan will use to try to distort the truths of God? It seems evident that from the beginning, Satan has been counting on us to mess up the very idea of love. If we cannot grasp the idea of love, we cannot understand the idea of God and we cannot fulfill the

basic requirement of loving other people. In fact, the very concept of love is so critical to humanity that it may be the only thing Satan needs to distort.

Once I was speaking to a group of young people and asked them to define the word love for me. As you can imagine, many definitions were offered. Some described a "butterfly" feeling they got in the stomach when someone they were attracted to walked into their presence. Some described the idea of love as tolerance. Some described it as sex. Some described it as some sort of arrangement.

The book of Job recounts occurrences in an early time in history when Satan was counting on Job to be confused about what love is and what it is not. Satan had already told God what he was attempting to do: namely, to get Job (or humankind) to believe that love means you give humans stuff, you keep them well, you make their lives easy. God, at that moment, apparently decided to put Job on display for the universe to observe.

This may seem like a place that you and I might want to be in, but this battle got ugly fast and Job either knew what love was all about or he did not. We know the rest of the story. We know that Job did not curse God; he seemed to actually understand what love was and what it wasn't. He seemed to know, somehow, that he might be on display—a test case, perhaps.

What do I understand about the love of God? What do I insist that God be or do to prove that He loves me? What conditions have I given to God?

From the oldest book of the Bible, we must come to the conclusion that Satan hopes to distort the idea of what it means to be loved by God. He wants me to believe that hard times and suffering mean that God has abandoned me. This is not true. Satan wants me to believe that a terminal illness means that God is not listening, when the reality may be not only that God is listening, but also that the entire heavenly realm is on the edge of their thrones. Satan desires nothing more than to get Christians to distort the meaning of love.

God, help me, as I live in your world and your Word, to define love as you define love and to rest in the fact that, even though I do not understand you, I can trust you because of your love for me.

N

True North: God is love and defines love.

_____

_____

_____

_____

_____

_____

_____

_____

_____

_____

Thought for Day 10

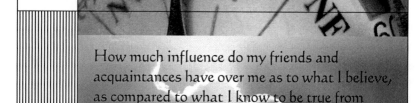

How much influence do my friends and acquaintances have over me as to what I believe, as compared to what I know to be true from Scripture?

Job 2:11–13 (NIV)

11 WHEN JOB'S THREE FRIENDS, ELIPHAZ THE TEMANITE, BILDAD THE SHUHITE AND ZOPHAR THE NAAMATHITE, HEARD ABOUT ALL THE TROUBLES THAT HAD COME UPON HIM, THEY SET OUT FROM THEIR HOMES AND MET TOGETHER BY AGREEMENT TO GO AND SYMPATHIZE WITH HIM AND COMFORT HIM.

12 WHEN THEY SAW HIM FROM A DISTANCE, THEY COULD HARDLY RECOGNIZE HIM; THEY BEGAN TO WEEP ALOUD, AND THEY TORE THEIR ROBES AND SPRINKLED DUST ON THEIR HEADS.

13 THEN THEY SAT ON THE GROUND WITH HIM FOR SEVEN DAYS AND SEVEN NIGHTS. NO ONE SAID A WORD TO HIM, BECAUSE THEY SAW HOW GREAT HIS SUFFERING WAS.

God seems to have carefully laid out the major schemes of Satan in Job, the oldest book in the Bible. First, we need to recognize that there is a real battle going on; that Satan is a real roaring lion who roams the earth looking for those he can devour. If we understand this and adjust our lives to this fact, we will be careful as to how we live, how we spend our time and our resources.

Second, it seems that Satan has taken the very core idea of God—which is love—and tried to distort it. He has

tried to get us to believe that we are only in the will of God when God gives us what we want and makes our lives easy.

Third, throughout most of this book of Scripture we see Satan using Job's friends to try to get Job to embrace his lies. These are not just acquaintances; these men are good friends. The majority of the book of Job is a description of what these three understand and how they use their distorted reality to try to "help" Job.

These three friends are really no different from many of our friends today. If we were in trouble, they would come, sit with us, pile ashes on their heads, and mourn with us. (Unless they're Swedish; we Swedes don't pile ashes on our heads!) They would demonstrate their friendship and give us loving advice. The problem, at least in this case, is that these three friends really did not have a clue as to what God was doing. Their advice was flat-out wrong. They began to tell Job that God must be paying him back for the secret wrongs he must have been committing. They had no idea of the battle, no idea of what Satan was up to, no idea of what love was all about.

Not only did they not have any idea of the reality of what was happening around them, but they were also more than willing to share their false and mistaken ideas, all the while wrapping them in as much human compassion and understanding as they could.

Well, no matter how you wrap it; three out of four of Job's friends—his good friends—were just plain wrong. They did not understand, even though they had good intentions, and thereby made the rough time that Job was going through even rougher. I see no difference today. Today, we see polls for everything, democratically controlled churches and people who make decisions based on a here-and-now understanding. In reality, most people do not know God or the ways of God, let alone get involved as front-line soldiers in the invisible spiritual war.

When the majority rules on an issue, it only means that the majority rules. It never means that the majority is necessarily right or wrong. God is always right and He is leading His troops today. There will be ugly moments that we do not totally understand, yet we need to remain firm in standing with the One we know, no matter where the tide of popular opinion tries to push us.

Is it possible that some of your closest friends—good friends—do not have a clue and that you are listening to them way too much? How can you adjust your life to hear the voice of God over the noise of the majority?

N

True North: A majority opinion may not have anything to do with truth.

_____

_____

_____

_____

_____

_____

_____

_____

Thought for Day 11

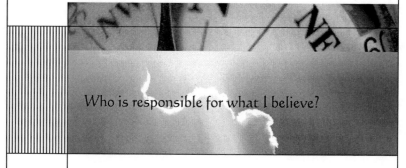

Who is responsible for what I believe?

Job 42:1–6 (NIV)

1 Then Job replied to the Lord:

2 "I know that you can do all things; no plan of yours can be thwarted.

3 You asked, 'Who is this that obscures my counsel without knowledge?' Surely I spoke of things I did not understand, things too wonderful for me to know.

4 You said, 'Listen now, and I will speak; I will question you, and you shall answer me.'

5 My ears had heard of you, but now my eyes have seen you.

6 Therefore I despise myself and repent in dust and ashes."

After we realize that there is an actual war, and after we see that the war is about the very idea of love, and after we see that even our closest friends could be some of our worst advisors, we need to clearly see this final point in the book of Job.

Toward the end of this book, it seems that Job has sorted it out. It seems that he came to a good conclusion: that

God could be God and that if He wanted to beat on Job, so be it.

In reality, though, that is not what was happening. In fact, when Job thought he had gotten it, he really did not get it, and God had to miraculously intervene to help him see that he did not yet understand. For several chapters God asks Job questions like, "Can you catch a crocodile" (41:1) and "Are you the one who makes the hawk soar and spread its wings to the south?"(39:26). In fact, it seems as if God went on forever asking Job questions whose answers indicated that Job was indeed only Job and God was God.

God seemed to be making a very powerful point in this old book. It could be that no matter what happens, our understanding will always be a limited understanding. It could be that we need to be careful who shapes our ideas and thoughts about God, and even be careful as to what we begin to conjure up. Still, I think the last point in this book—the point that really seems unique—is the moment when Job had the opportunity to blame his friends for what he believed. God asked Job, "Who is this that questions my wisdom with such ignorance?" (42:3). Yet, Job did not blame them. Instead, he did what any person of real character does: He took ownership of what he believed.

I am not sure, if given the opportunity, that I would take ownership and responsibility for all I believe. I would love to blame my family, my church, bad people, Hollywood, friends, and so on. I would love to play the blame game and be exonerated from my own bad choices. Yet, in this old book, the final lesson I see Job deliver is one of personal responsibility. Very simply, Job understood that he was responsible for what he believed.

One day I will stand before God, and I too will be held to account for what I did, what I believed, what I said. I have choices in life, and I can listen to the voice of God or to the voice of Dr. Phil, Oprah, or my pastor. In the end, though, either I will have believed right or I will have been wrong.

Right or wrong, I will stand before God alone and give an account (of course, my advocate Jesus will be there!). I need to dedicate myself to really understanding and being ready to take responsibility for what I believe and do.

True North: I am responsible for what I believe.

_____

_____

_____

_____

_____

_____

_____

_____

_____

_____

Thought for Day 12

What acceptable ways have I given Satan to deceive me with?

Genesis 3:1–7 (NIV)

1 Now the serpent was more crafty than any of the wild animals the Lord God had made. He said to the woman, "Did God really say, 'You must not eat from any tree in the garden?'"

2 The woman said to the serpent, "We may eat fruit from the trees in the garden,

3 But God did say, 'You must not eat fruit from the tree that is in the middle of the garden, and you must not touch it, or you will die.'"

4 "You will not surely die," the serpent said to the woman.

5 "For God knows that when you eat of it your eyes will be opened, and you will be like God, knowing good and evil."

6 When the woman saw that the fruit of the tree was good for food and pleasing to the eye, and also desirable for gaining wisdom, she took some and ate it. She also gave some to her husband, who was with her, and he ate it.

7 Then the eyes of both of them were opened, and they realized they were naked; so they sewed fig leaves together and made coverings for themselves.

What is the reality here?

Satan, once again lying about life and God.

I would think that when we encounter Satan, when we encounter the best, we would have a good excuse for our failure. Yet this is not the case.

I would expect that because God is sovereign, I am not really responsible for the stupid things I do, because I never really had a choice. Once again, this passage from Genesis proves otherwise.

I would like to believe that if God really was love, he would not really punish. This too is a lie from Satan himself.

What happened in the garden is probably more typical than extraordinary. Satan approaches Eve in an acceptable way, as a creature of the garden (a beautiful serpent), and begins to cast a shadow on God's word. He has Eve take the very word of God and change His statements into a question. He asks her if God really said that you must not eat any of the fruit of the garden. This is certainly a wonderful technique if you want to confuse what was already well understood.

We know that Eve understood God, because she told the serpent what God had said. She told the serpent what God meant, only to have Satan directly contradict what God had said. Satan told Eve that she would not die.

On what authority did Satan say this? Do we ever listen to people just because of their smoothness, authority, and command of our language?

When was the last time we recognized the devious ways of Satan in his attempts to have us question God's word or, even worse, disagree with God's word?

Could this be happening today? To me? What defenses
do I have in place?

N
*True North: Satan studies us and finds ways we
find acceptable to destroy us with.*

_____

_____

_____

_____

_____

_____

_____

_____

_____

_____

_____

_____

_____

_____

_____

Thought for Day 13

Do I actually lead when I know what is right, or do I give in to keep the (apparent) peace?

Genesis 3:6 (NIV)

6 WHEN THE WOMAN SAW THAT THE FRUIT OF THE TREE WAS GOOD FOR FOOD AND PLEASING TO THE EYE, AND ALSO DESIRABLE FOR GAINING WISDOM, SHE TOOK SOME AND ATE IT. SHE ALSO GAVE SOME TO HER HUSBAND, WHO WAS WITH HER, AND HE ATE IT.

Eve gave in to the rhetoric and logic of Satan. Satan made it seem like it was wise and appropriate to go against what God had said. He somehow made it logical to ignore God's directives and live in the realm of human understanding.

Adam, the man, did not even seem to care. He apparently just went along with whatever Eve wanted him to do. Could this have been the first "yes, dear" in history? Could this have been the first recorded instance of a man not really paying attention to what was going on in his own family?

It seems evident here that Eve thought she was doing something right. It might have been a good idea for her to go and talk it over with Adam and for Adam to take a stand against Satan. But, of course, it did not happen that way. Adam, for whatever reason, grabbed the fruit

and abdicated his leadership role, concentrating instead on whatever else was on his mind at that time.

This is not a good time in history: the doubting of God, the direct disobedience of Eve, the secondhand disobedience of Adam. There could have been a pre-bite discussion between Adam and Eve, or even a checking-in with God about this idea or for clarification. Sadly, none of this happened. The result affected the rest of history.

I am not sure that much is different today. Often the women of the household are left to make decisions alone, while the men are buried in their newspapers, watching sports, or out on the golf course. Often, even when we men are physically present, we are absent mentally; we "yes, dear" ourselves right into disaster.

God has a design for man and marriage. God expects us to listen to Him, and when we disagree with Him or do not understand Him, He expects us to come to Him and talk it over. He expects husbands and wives to talk, to communicate, and to hold each other to a high regard for what God has said.

Satan, in contrast, is on the other side of this issue. He is busy, once again, trying to isolate us, trying to get us to listen to our own logic and to distort what God has said even though, at one time, we knew what He said.

This war is intense and the consequences are great. What must I do today to make sure I do not make the same mistakes Adam and Eve made?

 True North: My feelings, logic, and understanding will let me down. I must listen to God in spite of them.

BEYOND THE COMPASS: Learning to See the Unseen

Thought for Day 14

God is sovereign, so isn't He responsible for my actions?

Genesis 3:8–13 (NIV)

8 THEN THE MAN AND HIS WIFE HEARD THE SOUND OF THE LORD GOD AS HE WAS WALKING IN THE GARDEN IN THE COOL OF THE DAY, AND THEY HID FROM THE LORD GOD AMONG THE TREES OF THE GARDEN.

9 BUT THE LORD GOD CALLED TO THE MAN, "WHERE ARE YOU?"

10 HE ANSWERED, "I HEARD YOU IN THE GARDEN, AND I WAS AFRAID BECAUSE I WAS NAKED; SO I HID."

11 AND HE SAID, "WHO TOLD YOU THAT YOU WERE NAKED? HAVE YOU EATEN FROM THE TREE THAT I COMMANDED YOU NOT TO EAT FROM?"

12 THE MAN SAID, "THE WOMAN YOU PUT HERE WITH ME—SHE GAVE ME SOME FRUIT FROM THE TREE, AND I ATE IT."

13 THEN THE LORD GOD SAID TO THE WOMAN, "WHAT IS THIS YOU HAVE DONE?" THE WOMAN SAID, "THE SERPENT DECEIVED ME, AND I ATE."

Now Adam is talking. He is trying to defend his inaction. When faced with God calling him on his disobedience, Adam tries to throw the "sovereignty" argument at God.

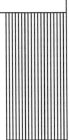

You remember that Job, the oldest book in the Bible, ends with Job accepting personal responsibility for what he believed. Well, now we are given an example of one who does not want to take responsibility for his actions. In fact, Adam says that the woman you put here with me—the woman whom you gave me, the one you provided to help me—is the problem. In this one statement, Adam implicates both God and Eve while trying to play the victim.

It did not work. As we learned with Job, God held Adam accountable for the decision he had made. He did not accept the argument that because God had given him Eve, God was responsible. He did not accept the argument that Eve was to blame. God made Adam own up to his decision.

We need to realize that a human, as long as he or she lives, has choice. It is indeed one of the great mysteries of life, but it is true nevertheless. In fact, the Bible clearly teaches that God is sovereign and that human-kind has choice. Though these things seem impossible, they are true. In my spiritual arrogance, I want to reduce these teachings to something that makes sense to me, something I can understand, but it is impossible to do so. Therefore, I must take the choices I have seriously while understanding that no matter what I do, God is, God does, and God will do.

This is one of the great mysteries of life, but it is clearly displayed in the lives of Adam, Eve, and Satan. I will stand before God one day and perhaps be tempted to blame my culture, my environment, or my friends. He will not allow such arguments. I will be held accountable for my actions, and I am responsible for what I believe and what I do with what I believe.

When I taught fifth grade, many years ago, I used to tell my students that while they were alive they would always have choice; I would challenge them to find a time when they did not. Often, students would come and boast that they had found a time or situation where they did not have choice. For example, they would talk of not having a choice if a robber had a gun to your head and was demanding your wallet—until I pointed out that you do indeed have a choice, as bad as it is: either give up your wallet or take a bullet to your head.

The only time you will have no choices is when God Almighty takes them away from you. Choice is a gift that, for now, can be used to bring glory to Him or render your life irrelevant.

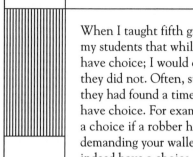 *True North: God is sovereign and I am responsible for my own choices.*

Thought for Day 15

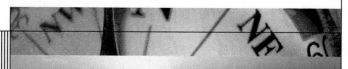

Am I allowing God to do anything in my life that will prove to those around me that He is God and that I am His servant?

1 Kings 18:30–35 (NIV)

30 THEN ELIJAH SAID TO ALL THE PEOPLE, "COME HERE TO ME." THEY CAME TO HIM, AND HE REPAIRED THE ALTAR OF THE LORD, WHICH WAS IN RUINS.

31 ELIJAH TOOK TWELVE STONES, ONE FOR EACH OF THE TRIBES DESCENDED FROM JACOB, TO WHOM THE WORD OF THE LORD HAD COME, SAYING, "YOUR NAME SHALL BE ISRAEL."

32 WITH THE STONES HE BUILT AN ALTAR IN THE NAME OF THE LORD, AND HE DUG A TRENCH AROUND IT LARGE ENOUGH TO HOLD TWO SEAHS OF SEED.

33 HE ARRANGED THE WOOD, CUT THE BULL INTO PIECES AND LAID IT ON THE WOOD. THEN HE SAID TO THEM, "FILL FOUR LARGE JARS WITH WATER AND POUR IT ON THE OFFERING AND ON THE WOOD."

34 "DO IT AGAIN," HE SAID, AND THEY DID IT AGAIN. "DO IT A THIRD TIME," HE ORDERED, AND THEY DID IT THE THIRD TIME.

35 THE WATER RAN DOWN AROUND THE ALTAR AND EVEN FILLED THE TRENCH.

What was Elijah thinking? Or perhaps we should ask, what did he understand?

I think that Elijah understood something that we so easily forget. This was not about being right or wrong, this was not about exonerating Elijah, this was not about putting a bad king and his followers in their place. This event, being played out on the turf of this earth and transmitted to the heavens, was one of those wonderful and rare moments in history when man did it right.

I cannot imagine the CEO of a Christian organization, in our day and age, making things as tough as possible so that when the end result happens, God alone can be glorified. We can't imagine marching so boldly into the impossible, knowing that either God will show up and accomplish the task, or we will look like total fools and failures.

Yet, Elijah—minus the feasibility studies, minus the censuses and polls, minus the long-range plans—steps into the spotlight of the universe, and for a moment the universe holds its collective breath.

The thing I do understand a bit is the heart of Elijah. Elijah prayed to God and asked God to answer his prayer; he asked God to prove this day that He was God and that Elijah was, well, just God's servant.

Within moments, God answered that prayer. With some spectacular fireworks, God sent a consuming fire to take care of business. I am certain that all who were in attendance and all the heavenly hosts that were privy to such earthly happenings were amazed at God being God.

What do I need to do as a leader to get myself to this same point? What do I need to do to be more concerned with God showing that He is God and less concerned with how I am going to make it happen? Would I dare douse the altars I am working on today? Would I ever

consider gathering the faithful, pointing out the impossible, and then proceeding?

If I knew what Elijah knew, I would! If I understood my role as Elijah understood his role, I would. If I were an intimate warrior, I would, because I would know that in the end the only thing that really matters is that God is glorified and that I would have had a chance, even if for only a brief time, to be His servant.

True North: I exist to glorify God.

Thought for Day 16

What would I need to know and believe to allow me to march boldly to my death rather than recant what I believe?

Daniel 3:19–23 (NIV)

19 Then Nebuchadnezzar was furious with Shadrach, Meshach and Abednego, and his attitude toward them changed. He ordered the furnace heated seven times hotter than usual

20 And commanded some of the strongest soldiers in his army to tie up Shadrach, Meshach and Abednego and throw them into the blazing furnace.

21 So these men, wearing their robes, trousers, turbans and other clothes, were bound and thrown into the blazing furnace.

22 The king's command was so urgent and the furnace so hot that the flames of the fire killed the soldiers who took up Shadrach, Meshach and Abednego,

23 And these three men, firmly tied, fell into the blazing furnace.

What did these three guys understand? What would make sane people cling to something so powerfully that they would be willing to die rather than let it go?

Nebuchadnezzar was angry. These three trusted men had defied him publicly. These three amigos were respectful,

but insistent that they would not disobey God, no matter what human consequences they faced.

Nebuchadnezzar gave them a challenge they could not pass up. He threatened them with a furnace and then asked them what god was capable of delivering them from the king's hands. Nebuchadnezzar challenged the wrong men, for they had already decided that obedience to God was more important than understanding.

Once again, I can only imagine the host of heaven gathering to watch events unfold. Would the three humans actually give God a chance to work? Would these boys have the courage to follow through with the decision they undoubtedly had talked about in private? When the time came for them to actually face the flames, would they give in or march on?

They marched on! I wonder if the host of heaven, the angels, argued over who would go and protect and meet them in the fire (and perhaps get their autographs). I wonder what Shadrach, Meshach, and Abednego actu-ally experienced after the demonstration of their faith.

I may not know the specifics, but I do know that in the end, a self-proclaimed god-king was shown to be wrong on a world stage. I do know that on this day, the one who thought he was god proved beyond any doubt that he was not, and that the only true God was the one these three men knew and obeyed. I do know that God used these boys' obedience, in this most difficult time, to accomplish His purposes.

I can only imagine the high fives around heaven as Satan shrunk and God was glorified. I can only imagine the angels, perhaps led by an angel who would one day help guard Martin Luther, singing a chorus of "A Mighty Fortress Is Our God."

I much more easily imagine another scene, a scene in which these three gave in to the pressure, surrendered to their fears, and bowed before the threatening earthly king. This scene is too tragic to think of, its ramifications too vast—but it happens all the time.

Today, God has a plan. I will be a part of it if I have decided to spend time with Him and obey Him, regardless of the apparent cost. Today, heaven may rejoice over my obedience or cringe at my disregard. I wonder which it will be? I know that the choice is up to me.

True North: Obedience is more important than understanding.

_____

_____

_____

_____

_____

_____

_____

_____

_____

_____

_____

Thought for Day 17

How important is talking with God?
How much have I talked with Him today?

Daniel 6:21–22 (NIV)

21 DANIEL ANSWERED, "O KING, LIVE FOREVER!

22 MY GOD SENT HIS ANGEL, AND HE SHUT THE MOUTHS
OF THE LIONS. THEY HAVE NOT HURT ME, BECAUSE I WAS
FOUND INNOCENT IN HIS SIGHT. NOR HAVE I EVER DONE
ANY WRONG BEFORE YOU, O KING."

Daniel, though missing from the furnace episode, makes similar choices and obtains similar results. It is quite obvious that Daniel was a man of integrity. It appears that many in positions of power were out to grab Daniel's power, and that he enjoyed a privileged position with the king. This privileged position was no doubt earned by hard work, honesty, faithfulness, and other good actions and qualities.

When Daniel's enemies went to destroy him, they found that he did nothing wrong. Even in his most private moments, he did what was right. In his public moments, he did what was right. We know that to destroy him, eventually his enemies had to concoct an accusation that had to do with his God.

Daniel must have been amused, but he did not seem scared. I am not sure what I would have done. I think

that I might at least have closed my windows when I prayed, but Daniel made no apologies for his intimacy with God, and was willing to allow God either to allow him to die for this or to use it for His honor and glory.

I would love to get some information from Daniel and the likes of him who appear throughout the Scriptures. I would love to hear the mental debate that must have raged in their heads. I would love to hear what his friends were advising him, what his culture was saying, and what family actually thought of such boldness.

I do know that Daniel seemed rather unconcerned with the king's edict. I also know that this king, somehow, knew of Daniel's God and began hoping that Daniel was right; before he had Daniel thrown into the lions' den, he told Daniel that he hoped the God whom Daniel worshipped continually would rescue him.

Once again, what is happening in the universe? Are the angels once again assembling, the faithful that have gone before placing themselves once again to observe God work in the life of a faithful man?

I do not know, but I do know that Daniel, the man in the hot seat, was thrown into the lions' den and was shocked, I am sure, at what he found. All night long, as the king tossed and turned, Daniel played with the lions. Who knows what really happened? Perhaps Daniel rearranged the lions in order to have a soft bed or pillow. Perhaps he played fetch the bone. Perhaps he pretended he was a lion tamer.

We do not know, but we do know that God once again honored the faith of one of His children and that by morning, Daniel had shown this king who God really was.

I wonder how many situations I have tried to get out
of that would have shown my world who God is?
I wonder why I so often try to avoid the impossible and
the improbable when it is those two things that God
so often uses?

True North: You will sleep better in the middle of danger with God than in comfort apart from Him.

_____

_____

_____

_____

_____

_____

_____

_____

_____

_____

_____

_____

Thought for Day 18

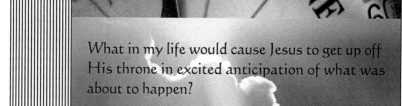

What in my life would cause Jesus to get up off His throne in excited anticipation of what was about to happen?

Acts 7:55–60 (NIV)

55 But Stephen, full of the Holy Spirit, looked up to heaven and saw the glory of God, and Jesus standing at the right hand of God.

56 "Look," he said, "I see heaven open and the Son of Man standing at the right hand of God."

57 At this they covered their ears and, yelling at the top of their voices, they all rushed at him,

58 Dragged him out of the city and began to stone him. Meanwhile, the witnesses laid their clothes at the feet of a young man named Saul.

59 While they were stoning him, Stephen prayed, "Lord Jesus, receive my spirit."

60 Then he fell on his knees and cried out, "Lord, do not hold this sin against them." When he had said this, he fell asleep.

In these verses, it seems that there is a bit of excitement on earth and in heaven. Stephen, obviously listening to God and confronting a people who do not want to be confronted, faces certain death. This death is not pleasant; this death is a death by stoning, at the hands of a crowd that knew how to make each stone give maximum punishment.

It would have been much easier for Stephen to write this crowd a note and mail it to them from a safe distance. It would certainly have been easier for Stephen if he had recognized their resistance to the truth and quit trying to shove the truth down their throats.

But it did not happen that way. Instead, Stephen was faithful to the message God gave him, no matter what. Once again, the host of heaven assembled on the edges of their thrones to watch what would happen.

This time, we are given a bit more information about what was happening. As Stephen started to feel the pain, it seems that he was guided by the Holy Spirit to look up. As he did, he saw Jesus. He not only saw Jesus, but saw Jesus no longer on the edge of His throne, but standing in front of it.

I do not know what else Stephen saw, but I bet you that as soon as he saw Jesus, the stones didn't seem so harsh anymore. I wish I knew if some sort of conversation took place between Stephen and Christ, or if Stephen could see the angels waiting to carry him, or if he could see the faithful throng cheering him.

I do not know.

But I do know this: Stephen caused some unusual activity in heaven!

I wonder if I will ever cause some unusual activity in heaven? I wonder if, when I die, Jesus will be on the edge of his throne or standing in anticipation?

Time will tell. <u>My obedience will determine my reception.</u>

 True North: God's plans will include suffering.

Beyond the Compass: Learning to See the Unseen

Thought for Day 19

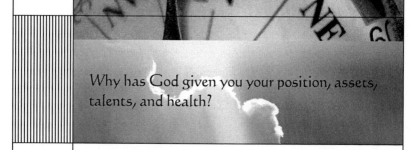

Why has God given you your position, assets, talents, and health?

Esther 4:13–17 (NIV)

13 HE SENT BACK THIS ANSWER: "DO NOT THINK THAT BECAUSE YOU ARE IN THE KING'S HOUSE YOU ALONE OF ALL THE JEWS WILL ESCAPE.

14 FOR IF YOU REMAIN SILENT AT THIS TIME, RELIEF AND DELIVERANCE FOR THE JEWS WILL ARISE FROM ANOTHER PLACE, BUT YOU AND YOUR FATHER'S FAMILY WILL PERISH. AND WHO KNOWS BUT THAT YOU HAVE COME TO ROYAL POSITION FOR SUCH A TIME AS THIS?"

15 THEN ESTHER SENT THIS REPLY TO MORDECAI:

16 "GO, GATHER TOGETHER ALL THE JEWS WHO ARE IN SUSA, AND FAST FOR ME. DO NOT EAT OR DRINK FOR THREE DAYS, NIGHT OR DAY. I AND MY MAIDS WILL FAST AS YOU DO. WHEN THIS IS DONE, I WILL GO TO THE KING, EVEN THOUGH IT IS AGAINST THE LAW. AND IF I PERISH, I PERISH."

17 SO MORDECAI WENT AWAY AND CARRIED OUT ALL OF ESTHER'S INSTRUCTIONS.

Esther thought she had it made. Elevated to queen! Food, parties, pampering, comfort, power, and all the other trimmings that come with royalty.

Then it happened.

She found out that she had been given this responsibility—this privilege, this position—for more than self-indulgent reasons. Her relative, Mordecai, came to her for help because there was a plot to kill all the Jews. He hit Esther with a line that has plagued good leaders for centuries since. He said, in verse 14, "What's more, who can say but that you have been elevated to this palace for just such a time as this?"

We know the rest of the story. Esther risked her life by approaching the king.

I can only imagine, yet again, the host of heaven gathering on the edges awaiting Esther's response. Would she do right? Would she allow God to use her to save the nation, or would God have to do it another way? Would she see her position as one given to her by God and to be used for His purposes, or would she ignore the seemingly obvious?

When she said, "If I must die, I am willing to die," I imagine the host of heaven let loose a collective roar of approval and triumph, for they understand the power of God that is unleashed in a dead servant's body and she had just proclaimed that she was dead to herself, no matter what the consequences.

I am no different from Esther. I too have been given privilege, position, power, and authority, but these gifts are not given to me for my own personal good. My Western mind wants me to think that all I have has been given to me for my personal enjoyment and gain, when in reality God has given me what I have to be used for His work, for His glory.

Today, I may find out why I am in the position I am. Today, I may be asked to give, to speak, to do something that only I am positioned or equipped to do. Today, the host of heaven may turn their collective attention toward me to see what I will do.

Will I be found faithful?

N
True North: God's blessings of position, power, and talent were not given to me for self-indulgent purposes.

_____

_____

_____

_____

_____

_____

_____

_____

_____

_____

_____

_____

_____

Thought for Day 20

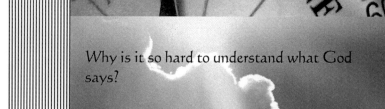

Why is it so hard to understand what God says?

Acts 1:9–11 (NIV)

9 AFTER HE SAID THIS, HE WAS TAKEN UP BEFORE THEIR VERY EYES, AND A CLOUD HID HIM FROM THEIR SIGHT.

10 THEY WERE LOOKING INTENTLY UP INTO THE SKY AS HE WAS GOING, WHEN SUDDENLY TWO MEN DRESSED IN WHITE STOOD BESIDE THEM.

11 "MEN OF GALILEE," THEY SAID, "WHY DO YOU STAND HERE LOOKING INTO THE SKY? THIS SAME JESUS, WHO HAS BEEN TAKEN FROM YOU INTO HEAVEN, WILL COME BACK IN THE SAME WAY YOU HAVE SEEN HIM GO INTO HEAVEN."

Sometimes you have to wonder what the angels are up to. What are they doing? What are they thinking? I often fall into a dream world of sorts, trying to figure out what is really going on and being frustrated with how limited my knowledge and understanding really are.

The scene described in these verses has to be one of the most interesting times in all of history. Here we have the apostles with Jesus, probably hoping that He will remain, that He will establish a kingdom, that He will continue to be here physically to guide and direct them. But He is leaving.

Jesus does not leave in any ordinary way. Rather, He leaves by, well, just leaving; just going up into the clouds and disappearing. I can imagine the disciples standing there with their mouths hanging open, their eyes squinting and their minds racing.

Then all of a sudden a couple of angels appear.

Where did they come from? Did Jesus tell them on the way up to go and disperse the crowd? Were these angels that had just been in the area and given the assignment to become visible and say the obvious?

The angels must often shake their heads at us humans. We seem to comprehend the truth so slowly. These angels came back and asked a question that implies that the disciples and the others there were not really listening when Jesus was on earth. In fact, they seem amazed at the humans' confusion. From their perspective, they knew what was going on. Jesus was leaving, but not forever. Jesus would be back. In fact, he will be back shortly, and will come back the same way he left: in the clouds.

It seems that this is well understood by all but the humans.

What else is well understood well except by humans? What else is there that I should know, that has been clearly revealed to me that still bothers me, that I don't "get"? What would angels ask me about if God allowed them to be visible and audible for a moment?

Sometimes I just don't get it. I need to spend whatever ponder time is necessary to really get it.

 True North: God is older than you, smarter than you, and loves you. You can trust Him.

Beyond the Compass: Learning to See the Unseen

Thought for Day 21

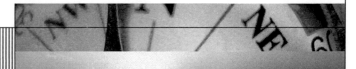

After my life on earth is over, will God allow me to be with Him forever? How do I know?

Revelation 20:11–15 (NIV)

11 Then I saw a great white throne and him who was seated on it. Earth and sky fled from his presence, and there was no place for them.

12 And I saw the dead, great and small, standing before the throne, and books were opened. Another book was opened, which is the book of life. The dead were judged according to what they had done as recorded in the books.

13 The sea gave up the dead that were in it, and death and Hades gave up the dead that were in them, and each person was judged according to what he had done.

14 Then death and Hades were thrown into the lake of fire. The lake of fire is the second death.

15 If anyone's name was not found written in the book of life, he was thrown into the lake of fire.

This is the reality yet to come. God makes it quite clear that in the end, He wins.

He makes it clear that in the end, all will stand before Him. He makes it clear that unless your name is written in the book of life, you will be among the forever punished.

These are not things that the Bible leaves to our imagination. These are the truths that are revealed and will be a reality for all humankind.

When the religious leader Nicodemus came to Jesus at night, he did not even know the right question to ask. Jesus, being God, knew what Nicodemus wanted to know and answered the question he never asked.

What Nicodemus wanted to know was the same thing all humankind has wanted to know from the beginning: How is it that, when this world is over and I face God, I will be able to face Him as my Father instead of my Judge?

Jesus told Nicodemus that in order for him to make things right with God, he needed to be "born again." He explained to Nicodemus that there must be a time in your life when you realize your sin and place your faith in what Jesus did for you on the cross.

John 3:16–17 (NLT)

16 FOR GOD LOVED THE WORLD SO MUCH THAT HE GAVE HIS ONE AND ONLY SON, SO THAT EVERYONE WHO BELIEVES IN HIM WILL NOT PERISH BUT HAVE ETERNAL LIFE.

17 GOD SENT HIS SON INTO THE WORLD NOT TO JUDGE THE WORLD, BUT TO SAVE THE WORLD THROUGH HIM.

For those who have been forgiven, there came a time in their lives when they understood that their personal sin has separated them from God, and that the only payment acceptable to God is that of the death of His

son, Jesus. Those who have placed their trust, their only hope, in what Jesus has done for them will be forgiven. Those who have tried to make it on their own will pay for their sins on their own. It is as Paul tells us:

Romans 3:28–30 (NLT)

28 So we are made right with God through faith and not by obeying the law.

29 After all, is God the God of the Jews only? Isn't he also the God of the Gentiles? Of course he is.

30 There is only one God, and he makes people right with himself only by faith, whether they are Jews or Gentiles.

There is only one God. There is only one way that He makes people right with Himself.

The angels just may be on the edge of their seats waiting for your response to this invitation.

 True North: No one will brag about being in heaven. We will be there only by the grace of God.

Final Thoughts

If I am traveling somewhere, I need directions. Even though I am now more than fifty years old, I still tend to get into the car, start driving, and attempt to get where I am going using my own "instincts" to find my way. I can almost guarantee that if I am supposed to travel west, I will turn east and travel for quite a while before I admit that I am going in the wrong direction.

I am much better off when someone who has been where I am going gives me directions: for example, go west on such-and-such a street; when you get to a particular intersection, turn north and continue to travel until . . . .

These directions are possible only because there is a true north. No matter where I am in the neighborhood, country, or world, north is north. There is no discussion on the matter, no debate. I can count on it—and if I know where it is, I can get to where I am going by listening to those who also know where true north and my final destination are.

At the many "intersections" of life, I need to trust the directions of those who have already been there, who know the way and are guided by something or someone that will never change. My "instincts" normally do not help me find my way. I need to learn both to ask for directions and to actually write them down and follow them.

Traveling through this life is also traveling somewhere. I often do not know how to get where I know I am going. I know that I am to glorify God. I know that I am headed to live with the King forever. I know that my life, if lived in the context of its creation, is headed toward a marvelous significance. In this book, you will read of those who knew that the directions from God were more than suggestions; they were and are the very words that have guided millions through some of life's most interesting situations.

Proverbs 3:5–6 (NLT)

5 Trust in the Lord with all your heart; do not depend on your own understanding.

6 Seek his will in all you do, and he will show you which path to take.

Isaiah 26:8 (NLT)

8 Lord, we show our trust in you by obeying your laws; our heart's desire is to glorify your name.

1 Corinthians 15:58 (NLT)

58 So, my dear brothers and sisters, be strong and immovable. Always work enthusiastically for the Lord, for you know that nothing you do for the Lord is ever useless.

Silver Birch Ranch
"To Know Christ and To Make Him Known"

Silver Birch Ranch has been serving our nation's youth since the summer of 1968. Its unique location allows children and families to enjoy swimming, horseback riding, white water rafting and more, while being challenged to understand and respond to God's plan for their lives.

Silver Birch Ranch also hosts year-round conferences and retreats for churches, and a Bible college, the Nicolet Bible Institute.

Silver Birch Ranch has many materials to help you in your effort to be intimate with God and family. Through the Omega Force program, you can receive materials that will help you with your personal walk with God, and remind you to live your life with "no regrets."

For information about Silver Birch Ranch, Nicolet Bible Institute, and the Omega Force program, please visit our web site at www.silverbirchranch.org.

If you are interested in inviting Dave Wager as a speaker for your special event, please contact him at Silver Birch Ranch, N6120 Sawyer Lake Road, White Lake, WI 54491, or by email at dave.wager@silverbirchranch.org.

Grace Acres Press products and services bring joy to your heart and life. Visit us at www.GraceAcresPress.com.

Upcoming titles in this series:
Beyond the Deception: Learning to Defend the Truth
Beyond the Expectation: Learning to Obey
Beyond the Feeling: Learning to Listen

Also available from Grace Acres Press:

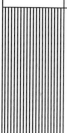

Beyond the Resistance:
Learning to Face Adversity
by Dave Wager
Foreword by Ian Leitch
$11.95

Improve your leadership effectiveness by growing closer to the heart of God using this 21-day guided journal.

Strengthened by Grace:
A Systematic Theology Handbook
by Richard E. Wager
Foreword by Art Rorheim
$19.95

Easy-to-use theology reference for your home. Prepares you to give reasons and rationale for your beliefs.

For orders or information about quantity discounts or reprints,
Call 888-700-GRACE (4722)
Fax (303) 681-9996
Email info@GraceAcresPress.com